W9-BVM-287

HIGHWAY 33
... from Ojai to Cuyama

A Traveler's Guide to California's Scenic Highway 33

... from Ojai to Cuyama

Written by E.R. "Jim" Blakley

Edited by Jeanine Moret

Published by Shoreline Press, Santa Barbara, California

Copyright 2004 by Jim Blakley

All rights reserved

No part of this book shall be reproduced in any form whatsoever without written permission of the publisher.

Published by: Shoreline Press
                 P.O. Box 3562
                 Santa Barbara, California 93130

Distributed by: Pacific Books
                 2573 Treasure Drive
                 Santa Barbara, California 93105
                 (805) 687-8340

ISBN 1-885375-12-3

First edition/ First printing

Photographs by Jim Blakley (pages 26, 36), Chris Danch (page 17), Jeanine Moret (pages 4, 19, 21, 22, 24, 28, 30, 32, 35, 37, 40, 41, 42, 44), Wayne Goldwyn (cover, pages 3, 7, 14) Postcards, by unknown photographers, from the collection of John Fritsche (pages 8, 9, 10, 11, 12, 13); Photo by unknown photographer from Blakley Archive (page 27)
Book design and layout by Jeanine Moret

Printed in China

DEDICATION

I wish to dedicate this book to my wonderful wife MAE,
who for over fifty years made it possible for me to collect and study information
about the Santa Barbara and Ventura counties backcountry
of Los Padres National Forest.

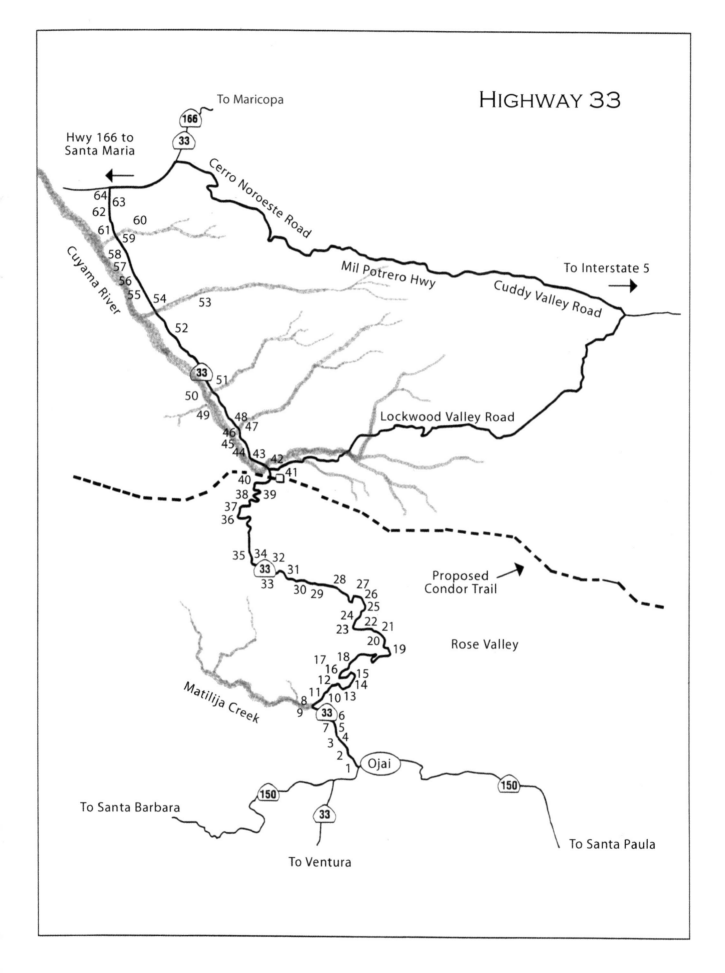

HIGHWAY 33

To Maricopa

166

Hwy 166 to
Santa Maria

33

Cerro Noroeste Road

64 63
62
60
61
59
58
57
56
55 54
53
52

Mil Potrero Hwy

Cuddy Valley Road

To Interstate 5

Cuyama River

33 51
50
49 48
47
46
45
44 43 42
40 41
38 39
37
36

Lockwood Valley Road

Proposed
Condor Trail

35 34 32
33 31
33 30 29
28 27
26
25
24 22 21
23 20
19

Rose Valley

17 18
16 15
12 14
11 13
8 10
9 33 6
7 5
4
3 2
1 Ojai

Matilija Creek

150

To Santa Barbara

33

150

To Ventura

To Santa Paula

LIST OF SITES

INTRODUCTION

California Scenic Highway 33 begins in Ventura at a junction with Highway 101 and runs north toward Ojai. At a junction on the outskirts of Ojai, the route forks off in a northwesterly direction as Maricopa Highway. On its way to Maricopa, the 33 winds up the narrow Sespe Gorge, over Pine Mountain Summit, and northward along the austere upper Cuyama Valley. The last 14 miles before Maricopa, the highway descends from 2,968 feet into the 3-figure elevations of the San Joaquin Valley. It runs the length of the valley in segments, connecting tiny towns like McKittrick, Avenal, and Volta before petering out south of Stockton.

This guide describes the historical and topographical features of the most scenic section of Highway 33; from the start of the Maricopa Highway west of Ojai to its junction with Highway 166 east of Cuyama.

The route was discussed for more than 35 years before it was constructed in the 1930's for $1.8 million. Residents of Santa Barbara and Ventura hoped to lure tourists from the Central Valley to coastal vacation spots, and residents of the hot San Joaquin and Cuyama Valleys wanted beach access. In 1911, oil barons from Maricopa and Taft led a caravan to Ventura to stir up interest in a Maricopa highway. However, it took another 15 years for officials from Ventura, Santa Barbara, and Kern counties to team up with local politicians and secure the federal funds to begin designing the route.

The road shortened the trek between Carpinteria and Bakersfield by more than 100 miles. The project involved more than four years of almost continuous construction. Bonds had to be issued by Santa Barbara, Kern, and Ventura counties to complete the last seventeen mile segment, which includes the Sespe Gorge. In this section, 400 tons of explosives were used to blast millions of tons of dirt and solid rock. Up to 512 men at a time were employed at forty cents per hour.

The oil and gravel coated "Maricopa Road", as it was first known, opened with great fanfare on October 22, 1933. The celebration at the Wagy Ranch in the upper Cuyama Valley was attended by 35,000 people. The new road was formally designated a State Highway by the State Highway Commission on June 26, 1934.

The route's history can be traced back to the late 1800's, when homesteaders settled in the upper Sespe and Cuyama Rivers of the Ventura County backcountry. For some, the round trip to pay taxes at the county seat in San Buenaventura was a week's journey of over 300 miles. The "Ridge Route" from the Cuyama Valley went around Lake Elizabeth near what is now Palmdale. Some settlers braved the network of trails, frequented by bears and bandits, that ran up canyons and over ridges between the Sespe, Matilija, and Cuyama watersheds. Their ally and protector was J.D. Reyes.

Jacinto Damien Reyes was the eldest son of rancher Rafael Reyes, who homesteaded in the upper Cuyama Valley in 1855. As a forest ranger for the Cuyama District from 1900 to 1931, J.D. Reyes patrolled the backcountry on horseback, guiding and protecting travelers and homesteaders who used the mountain trails. In 1995, a 38 mile segment of Highway 33 was named the Jacinto Reyes Scenic Byway by the U.S. Forest Service. The Reyes family also left their name on Reyes Creek and Reyes Peak, and their descendants still ranch in the Cuyama Valley.

To travel the 33 with Jim Blakley is to experience this magical highway on many levels, thanks to his running commentary that interweaves landscape, anecdote, and natural history. We hope that this book will provide pleasure and insight to others who share our love of the local backcountry.

- Jeanine Moret

1 STARTING POINT:
MARICOPA ROAD AT HIGHWAY 150 ✎ MILEAGE = 0

The part of Highway 33 known as the Maricopa Road begins west of Ojai, at the junction of Highways 150 and 33. A large shopping center on the northwest corner marks the intersection where this tour begins. Turn left where you see signs for 33 North and the Maricopa Highway. If you have a mileage counter or odometer, zero it here and you can follow our "Mileage" numbers for the points of interest along the drive. For drivers who do not have an odometer, we have included highway marker numbers as reference points where they are available. These low white markers appear along the right hand side of the road, and are referred to in this guide as "Marker".

Highway sign and mileage marker along the Maricopa Road

Along the route there are several businesses that provide food and refreshments, but the only gas station between Ojai and Cuyama is at the Santa Barbara Pistachio Company store, 53 miles beyond Ojai.

As you drive the length of the Maricopa Road, you will cross three county lines. Most of the route is within Ventura County, but in the upper Cuyama Valley it crosses briefly into Santa Barbara and San Luis Obispo counties. In these two counties, highway markers are used only once a mile, at best. For this reason we refer only to odometer mileage outside of Ventura county.

4

2 McDONALD CANYON AND CREEK   MILEAGE = .6

This little canyon, located in the foothills north of Ojai, has an intermittent creek which flows down through an area of homes and small farms. The creek is difficult to locate until it crosses under the highway, where a small white fence signals the presence of a culvert under the road. From this point on, McDonald Creek is visibly lined with trees and shrubs as it travels west. It flows through the Ojai Meadows Preserve before joining the Ventura River north of Meiners Oaks.

3 DEER LODGE   MILEAGE = 1.4

Deer Lodge is an informal dinner house, currently owned and managed by Terry Kenton. The lodge first opened in 1932, and was originally frequented by deer hunters who gathered to exchange notes and tips regarding good places to hunt. The lodge also dressed the kill and packaged the meat for the hunters.

Deer Lodge was once a popular gathering spot for hunters

The interior is decorated in a Western theme, with many trophy heads on display. There is a well-stocked bar featuring local beverages and wines. The restaurant serves exotic game meats such as venison, elk, boar and quail, along with more traditional fare. The Lodge is open daily for lunch and dinner, and holds a barbecue on Sunday afternoons. Live entertainment is featured on Wednesdays and weekends.

In the past, Deer Lodge was noted as a stopping place for motorcycle and bicycle groups preparing for or returning from a ride over Highway 33 to Cuyama.

4 COZY DELL CREEK ⌇ MILEAGE = 2.6 ⌇ MARKER = 13.73 (BRIDGE)

The highway runs along the east side of the Ventura River Valley for about 3 miles, over alluvial deposits of boulders and sandy clay that has washed down from the higher mountains to the northeast. This alluvial material obscures the underlying Sespe Red beds of the Oligocene, which are 30 million years old.

The first bridge on Highway 33 crosses over Cozy Dell Creek, though the bridge was long mislabeled as McDonald Creek. Near the head of this creek is the "type locality" of the Cozy Dell Shale formation; that is, the very place where Cozy Dell shale was first identified and named. Large areas of this shale are found along the route of Highway 33. The Cozy Dell shale lies beneath the Coldwater sandstone formation, and was formed in the upper Eocene Age some 37 million years ago.

Where Cozy Dell Creek joins the Ventura River, a red roofed house can be seen in a grove of orange trees to the left of the highway. This private property was once the location of the Chumash village of Matilija. The Matilija rock formation, canyon, and creek and were all named after this indigenous village.

More recently, the location became known as the site of the Lopez Adobe. Raphael Lopez built an adobe here in 1839 with the help of a handful of soldiers and Chumash people. It was constructed as an outpost, to prevent mountain Chumash from raiding the San Buenaventura Mission. Fifty years later Francisco Marcos Lopez filed a homestead claim on the site, and he received a patent on February 12, 1892. Members of the Lopez family lived in the adobe for well over 100 years. The orange grove, planted in 1915 and still thriving, was one of the first established in the Ojai Valley.

Along the sides of the highway are clumps of a grass growing as tall as two and a half feet. It is known as fountain grass, originally brought from Africa as an exotic garden plant but now spreading on its own. Mingled with the fountain grass is a large shrub known as Spanish broom, composed of bright yellow flowers clustered on almost leafless green stems. This plant belongs to a large group of invasive shrubs including Scotch broom and French broom. It was introduced from southern Europe, where it is cultivated extensively for its flowers, and has established itself all along Highway 33 in the lower elevations.

Fennel from the Mediterranean region, widely used in the cuisine of southern Europe, is also gaining ground along the margins of the native chaparral. It is closely related to poison hemlock, an herb that is found growing in disturbed chaparral areas.

5 BODEES BAR ⌇ MILEAGE = 2.7 ⌇ MARKER = 13.81

Just past the Cozy Dell bridge on the right side of the highway sits Bodees Bar, established in 1939 by Hiram Cormer. The original building was burned to the ground in 1952 by a fire that also took Mr. Cormer's life. Loyal friends and patrons helped his wife rebuild the bar, and she continued to operate it for many years as a meeting place for local residents. Recently it was open on weekends only, but at present it is completely closed.

About 250 feet past Bodees bar, at highway marker 14.10, you will note the first bedrock visible since the junction of Highways 33 and 150. These are cream colored beds of 40 million year old Coldwater sandstone, with deposits or bands of reddish brown sandstone. The red material fools a lot of people into believing it is Sespe rock, but it is Coldwater; and the beds are overturned or upside down from the way they were deposited. A large outcropping of the red Sespe-like formation occurs at marker 14.36, and continues until you reach the Friends packing house at Sheldon Creek.

6 FRIENDS PACKING HOUSE; COZY DELL TRAIL
MILEAGE = 3.5   ⌐   MARKER = 14.58

On the right hand side of the road stands an old wooden building with a loading dock; this is the former Friends Fruit Stand, now in use as a packing house.

The Sheldon family ranch across the highway from the building was one of the first orange groves planted in the Ojai area. After the opening of Highway 33, a stand was built to market the oranges. It was long noted as a stop to drink a glass of fresh squeezed orange juice and pick up a sack of oranges to take home. Eventually the stand was sold to the Friends Ranches, owned by an old Ojai family. Later the ownership passed to the Thatcher family, also long established in Ojai. They closed the retail operation but continue to pack oranges in season.

The Cozy Dell Trail starts on the south bank of Sheldon Creek next to the packing house. The trail follows the small creek upstream, then climbs the side of the canyon to reach a ridge crest where a great view of the western Ojai Valley can be enjoyed.

Just past the packing house, the first of the numerous Cozy Dell shale outcroppings along Highway 33 can be seen. On the right hand side, look for a light tan, crumbling shale bank striped with fine layers of sandstone. Across the road from the shale deposit is a private ranch road called Camino Cielo. This would have been the eastern terminus of a Forest Service road running along the Santa Ynez Mountain crest from Gaviota Hot Spring to Matilija Hot Springs, a distance of approximately fifty miles. The ambitious project was begun shortly after World War II, but was never completed.

7 SOPER'S GYMNASIUM   ⌐   MILEAGE = 3.9   ⌐   MARKER = 15.07

In 1925, Clarence "Pop" Soper constructed a gymnasium and training camp for prizefighters at his ranch on the west side of the Ventura River, across from the Cozy Dell trailhead. Several professional fighters trained at the camp, and local residents could watch the action for the sum of one dollar. Jack Dempsey was the first well known fighter to train at Soper's, while preparing for his match with Gene Tunney.

Pop's father, Philander Wallace Soper, originally homesteaded the site with his wife in 1875 and made coffins for a living. Clarence was born in 1881, and worked in Los Angeles for the Wells Fargo Company for over 20 years before returning to Ojai to take over the property. In 1938, R.H. Everett leased a part of the ranch from Pop Soper and constructed a number of cabins for visitors to the canyon. The rural resort was named "Ojala", a combination of "Ojai" and "Matilija". *Ojala* is also a Spanish expression meaning "I hope so!".

# 8 START OF THE VENTURA RIVER
MILEAGE = 4.4   MARKER = 15.44

The Ventura River officially starts at the confluence of two great branches of Matilija Creek, the north fork and the main fork. From this point of origin, the river flows southward approximately twenty miles to reach the Pacific Ocean just west of the city of Ventura.

For the next ten miles or so, Highway 33 will follow the North Fork of the Matilija, crossing it many times. A green "S. Matilija Road" sign marks the junction of the two creeks. This private road is locked a short distance from Highway 33, but it continues up the main fork to the spot where Matilija Dam was built in a narrows of the canyon. Over the years, the lake formed by the dam has filled with sediment. Recently it was decided to remove the dam so the endangered steelhead trout can swim to the upper reaches of the stream to spawn. Time will tell how effective this experiment will be in restoring the spawning grounds of the steelhead.

The Ventura River begins where the forks of Matilija Creek converge

Before Highway 33 was constructed, the narrows of the North Fork through the massive Matilija sandstone formation was an impassible route for vehicles. The original road northward from Ojai followed the main fork of Matilija Creek up to the west end of its narrows, where the dam was eventually built. At that point, the old road climbed up over the ridge that divides the canyons, then descended into the upper North Fork. The ridge portion of this road has been improved, and now serves as an access road to the upper regions of the main Matilija drainage.

⑨ MATILIJA HOT SPRINGS ⁀ MILEAGE = 4.4 ⁀ MARKER = 15.44

This magazine ad drew visitors to the resort

Matilija Canyon contains natural hot springs, and has been home to several different resorts over the years. The property surrounding the natural hot springs was first homesteaded in 1872 by J.W. Wilcox. He sold to R.M. Brown, who added a road, cabins, and a bathhouse; and hired a cook and attendants to serve the ailing guests. In 1877, Captain Gardner purchased the property. He added cottages, and named the resort "Matilija Hot Springs". The entire facility was destroyed by a flood in 1884.

In 1887 Abram Blumberg homesteaded land near the site of the former Matilija Hot Springs resort. Blumberg opened a resort called "Ojai Hot Springs" that featured a store, a dining room, and cottages. He claimed that the sulphur spring was 104 degrees, and good for a long list of physical problems. One of the springs was called "Fountain of Life". Another, called "Mother Eve", was reputed to contain certain minerals that cured many dread diseases. In 1893 he ran a daily stage to Ojai to transport visitors up the canyon to his resort. Members of the Blumberg

Postcards of the era promoted the healing powers of the mineral waters

family sold the property in 1901 to S.P. Creasinger. He added many expensive improvements and then went bankrupt, and the management was taken over by Sam Meyers. Finally, Ventura County purchased the resort in 1947 during the construction of Matilija Dam, since they knew that lake waters eventually would flood the site.

A turn-of-the-century postcard shows the stage that carried visitors to the springs

Just up the canyon, another resort was established in 1871 by Robert Lyons. It was known first as Cliff Glen, and later as Lyon's Springs. This resort was removed when the dam project was developed, even though the lake formed by the dam never reached that far up the canyon. Now great masses of a giant reed named *Arundu donax* choke the banks on either side of the creek where the Lyons resort once stood.

10 OJAI ROCK QUARRY   MILEAGE = 4.5   MARKER = 15.5

The sandstone visible in tall cliffs on both sides of the canyon is the type location of the Matilija Formation, deposited during the Eocene epoch some 55 million years ago. Near the quarry there is a road cut where some fossil seashells are exposed.

During the construction of Highway 33, rock debris from this area was found to be useful in many construction projects and a quarry was established. Some of this rock was used to build a tiny island off Mussel Shoals, a tiny coastal town north of Ventura. The island was then used as an oil drilling site.

11 MATILIJA CANYON ROAD AND BERRY FLAT
MILEAGE = 5.1   MARKER = 16.13 (BRIDGE)

Just after Highway 33 crosses a bridge on the North Fork of Matilija Creek, Matilija Canyon Road branches off on the left. It climbs steeply over a ridge and descends to continue up Matilija

Canyon. The road continues past several homes, to reach a locked gate and a parking area. From the gate, it continues on unpaved as a Forest Service administrative road, passing Juncal Lake and Dam to end at a junction with the Santa Ynez River road.

In the old days the road ran up the main fork of Matilija Creek past Matilija Hot Springs, through the narrows where the dam was later built, and finally split into two roads. The left fork continued into the upper regions of Matilija Creek, and the right fork climbed up and over a ridge to descend to the North Fork of Matilija Creek.

Berry Flat was at one time the furthest one could travel up the North Fork of the Matilija. It was the homestead of the Berry family, related by marriage to the Blumbergs of Wheeler's Hot Springs. Around the turn of the century, the Wheeler Tunnel was excavated to allow vehicles to reach Wheeler Hot Springs. When Highway 33 was constructed, the Wheeler Tunnel was destroyed and 3 new tunnels were excavated farther up the canyon.

12 WHEELER'S HOT SPRINGS
MILEAGE = 6.6   MARKER = 17.52

The highway passes through Juncal Formation rock strata until you reach Wheeler's Hot Springs, located on the Santa Ynez fault. Hot water ascends from deep within the earth to form the spring, which is really just a warm spring with a boiler to increase the water temperature.

Health seekers could continue up the canyon to Wheeler's Hot Springs

Wheeler Blumberg discovered the site in 1888 when he shot a deer on a hunting trip and it fell near the spring. Blumberg noted that the water was warm, and filed a homestead claim on the land. In 1894 he built a hotel for the public.

ENTRANCE TO WHEELER SPRINGS CANYON.   VENTURA COUNTY, CALIFORNIA.

Before Highway 33 was made, Wheeler's Hot Springs was the end of the road

In 1905, Etta Blumberg married Webb Wilcox and they purchased the resort. In 1913, they developed "Wilcox's Cottages" and a post office across the highway from the thermal spring. The six by seven foot building was featured in *Ripley's Believe It or Not* as the smallest post office in the United States. It served some 80 families in its heyday, and operated until 1962.

Wheeler's Hot Springs once boasted the smallest post office in the United States

Etta and Webb opened a restaurant across the highway from Wheeler's Hot Springs. For many years it was a favorite stopping place for Ojai locals as well as travelers along Highway 33. On weekends a large number of motorcyles could often be seen outside Wilcox's Grill.

In recent years, several owners have managed Wheeler's Hot Springs. The last owner had tax trouble and the government took over the property, which is so deeply in debt that no one is able to operate it.

13 HIGHWAY 33 TUNNELS ⤺ MILEAGE = 7.5

The original tunnel on the old road up the canyon was known as the Wheeler Tunnel. Travelers passed through it just before reaching Wheeler's Hot Springs. Wheeler Tunnel was demolished to make way for Highway 33, and three new tunnels were constructed through the steep-sided Wheeler Gorge.

The approach to the first tunnel is signaled by the dark colored Cretaceous rock to the left of the highway. It is a hard, brownish formation composed of sandstone and shale beds. The tunnel, reinforced with steel and concrete, curves as it passes under a rocky ridge. Running parallel with the highway on its left side is the Santa Ynez fault, which is considered the northern boundary of the Transverse Range.

After the first tunnel, a sign on the right of the highway marks the boundary of Los Padres National Forest and informs travelers that a "Forest Adventure Pass" is required to park along the road. Next come two tunnels very close together, with the creek crossing the highway between them and again after the last one. These bridges were refitted in 2001.

Road construction through this gorge was one of the most difficult parts of the Highway 33 project. Construction was begun by Merritt, Chapman and Scott on May 13, 1931. They completed the first of the tunnels in March

THE TUNNEL, WHEELERS HOT SPRINGS,
VENTURA COUNTY, CALIFORNIA.

The original tunnel was excavated around 1900

1932, at a cost of over $364,000. Work was completed on the other two tunnels in October of the same year.

Just past the third tunnel, a small spring flows down the rock wall on the right side of the highway (cover photo). Interesting water loving plants cling to the wet cliff face below the spring, which occurs on the Santa Ynez fault.

The tunnels mark the traveler's entry to Los Padres National Forest

14 WHEELER GORGE CAMPGROUND AND L.P.F.A. INFORMATION CENTER
Mileage = 8.2 d Marker = 19.10 (bridge)

Upon leaving Wheeler Gorge, you will notice that the gorge ends abruptly and the valley becomes more open. This is because you have just crossed the Santa Ynez fault and are once again within Cozy Dell shale, which is much softer than the Cretaceous rock that makes up the gorge. The original road used to circumvent the entire Wheeler Gorge by climbing up the left wall of the canyon at the start of the narrows and following the ridgeline. It then descended back into the valley at Wheeler Springs.

Wheeler Gorge Campground sits on the left side of the highway. Now a popular Forest Service campground, it was originally a Boy Scout camping area. The small stone building at the entrance was the scout camp headquarters. Shortly after Highway 33 was constructed, the scout camp was moved and the campground was opened to the public. There are many sites with stoves, tables, water, and restrooms. A campground host runs the facility for a private management company that leases it from the Forest Service.

Across the highway from the campground, the Forest Service built a fire station in 1935. The station is now considered obsolete and has been leased to the Los Padres Forest Association (L.P.F.A.), the Forest Service's official public information partner in the Los Padres region. The L.P.F.A. maintains an information center that provides maps and books related to the forest.

15 THREE LANDMARKS   ⌇ MILEAGE = 8.5 TO 9.1

A. BEAR CREEK BRIDGE
MILEAGE = 8.5   ⌇   MARKER = 19.36 (ON BRIDGE)

The highway crosses over Bear Creek, which flows into Matilija North Fork from the east. "Bear" is one of the most commonly used California place names, particularly in creeks and canyons. Gudde states, in his *California Place Names*, that there are over 5,000 references to "bear". Ventura County has at least eleven of them to its credit. The California grizzly has been extinct in Ventura County since 1905, and the common black bear has taken over the grizzly's range in many areas.

B. FINAL NORTH FORK CROSSING   ⌇   MILEAGE = 8.8

For the past few miles, the highway has been crossing back and forth over the North Fork of Matilija Creek. A short distance after crossing Bear Creek, the highway crosses the North Fork for the last time. The Wheeler Gorge Nature Trail, developed by the Los Padres Interpretive Association, begins on the right hand side of the highway just before this bridge. It follows along the north side of the creek through a riparian area, climbs up to a chaparral covered ridge top, and then loops back down to the bridge.

This bridge, the one over Bear Creek, and several others over the North Fork were built in 2000 and 2001 to replace the old wooden bridges dating from the original Highway 33 construction. The old bridges were starting to fall apart under the heavy traffic on the highway.

C. ELEVATION SIGN   ⌇   MILEAGE = 9.1   ⌇   MARKER = 19.99

A short distance past the second bridge is a sign marking 2000 feet elevation.

16 HOLIDAY GROUP CAMP   ⌇   MILEAGE = 9.5

The camp is located at the end of a short road behind a locked gate, and can be reserved for group use. Access is administered by the Forest Service through Wheeler Gorge Campground.

A large BBQ pit and a serving table are located at the center of the camping area, surrounded by a number of individual campsites with their own tables and iron grills. There is one pit toilet for the entire facility. There is no water available at the camp.

17 ORTEGA TRAIL   ⌒ MILEAGE = 10   ⌒ MARKER = 20.80

The Ortega Trail is designated by the Forest Service as OHV (Off Highway Vehicle) trail #23W08, and is popular with motorcyclists. It starts on the left hand side of Highway 33, a half mile beyond the Holiday Group Camp. From this trailhead, it ascends to the base of Ortega Hill and continues around the south side of the hill to a saddle at the head of Cherry Creek Canyon. At this saddle it joins the Upper North Fork trail from Matilija Canyon, and continues down Cherry Creek Canyon to the Sespe River and Highway 33.

The Ortega Trail was originally established as a winter route, providing an alternative to the high waters that used to make the Upper North Fork of Matilija Creek impassible during the rainy season. It was named for Ramon Ortega, who had a large ranch at Potrero Seco on the upper Sespe during the early 1800's. The trail provided an important thoroughfare between the northern "backcountry" and the southern "civilized" parts of Ventura County. This access is now provided by Highway 33.

18 BELLYACHE SPRING   ⌒ MILEAGE = 11.6   ⌒ MARKER = 22.37

Bellyache Spring is marked by the remains of a stone drinking fountain on the left side of the road. For many years, water was piped down from the spring, which is located in a small canyon to the north of Highway 33. The water fountain was constructed some time ago, but it no longer functions and vandalism has almost destroyed it.

Two stories are told of the naming of this spring. One account says that the Forest Service rangers from areas north and south of the spring used to meet and "bellyache" about how things were going in their parts of the forest. The other story is that drinking too much of the cold water would result in a bellyache.

If you look east across the canyon from the highway near the spring, you can see the remains of a fire lookout on the crest of Nordhoff Ridge just north of the city of Ojai. The top of Nordhoff Lookout was removed, but the base remains as a platform from which to observe the forest and the city of Ojai below. There is an administrative road with a locked gate that leads from Rose Valley Campground to the old tower site.

19 ROSE VALLEY ROAD   ⌒ MILEAGE = 15.3   ⌒ MARKER = 25.77

Four miles to the east along this Forest Service road lie Rose Valley Campground and Lake, and a beautiful, very tall waterfall. The road used to lead to Lion Campground, which was the trailhead for both the Sespe River Trail and the Gene Marshall Piedra Blanca National Recreation Trail. Lion Campground has been permanantly closed due to environmental concerns for the endangered red legged frog, arroyo toad and steelhead trout.

A large coniferous tree marks the Rose Valley Road turnoff. The tree is a lone representative of the bigcone Douglas-fir, commonly referred to as "bigcone-spruce", which will be seen in profusion as the highway gains altitude. On the surrounding hillsides are numerous chaparral shrubs such as wild cherry or islay, mountain holly or toyon, mountain mahogany, and yucca. The mountain mahagony is a sight in autumn, when it displays threadlike spiraling seed tails covered with a silver "fur" that catches the sunlight and lends the shrubs a distinctive glow.

20 PUERTO SUELO   MILEAGE = 16.2 TO 16.4

View from the Dry Lakes Trail with Pine Mountain Ridge visible on the right

The term *puerto suelo* is one of many variations on the Spanish word *puertezuelo*, which describes a pass that separates one drainage from another. In this case, the highway climbs out of the Matilija North Fork drainage and descends into the Sespe River valley. At the top of the divide on the west side of the highway, a firebreak climbs steeply to the ridgetop. It is known as the Dry Lakes Trail, and leads to the shallow depressions known as the Dry Lakes.

A good vantage point is at 16.7 miles, near the 26.75 highway marker. Looking southward down the canyon of Matilija North Fork, Divide Peak is visible in the Santa Ynez Range. On a clear day you can see the ocean and the Channel Islands. As you enter the Sespe drainage, the south face of Pine Mountain Ridge comes into view. At the base of the ridge, eroded reddish rock of the Sespe Formation can be seen in the valley that bears its name.

As the highway begins to descend from its high point, it passes massive beds of cream colored Matilija sandstone, which is soon replaced by dark gray Cozy Dell shale near the bottom of the grade. Across the river are red Sespe rocks, often with a covering of brownish Coldwater sandstone. The nearby Tule Creek fault influences the formations in this area.

21 BEAVER CAMPGROUND
MILEAGE = 17.6   MARKER = 28.07

The site of the former Beaver Campground is located on the bank of Sespe Creek, at the end of a very short paved road. The elevation is 3,300 feet. Prior to 1998 the campground had been closed due to storm damage. It was open only briefly, then was again closed in 1999 to protect the arroyo toads and steelhead trout. Many of the endangered toads were being crushed by cars driving into the campground. To prevent this, a gate was placed across the entrance road one tenth of a mile from Highway 33, and the facility has become a walk-in trailhead with no camping permitted.

From the former campground, the Middle Sespe Trail follows the north bank of the creek some eight miles to Piedra Blanca. Cottonwood trees line the riparian streambed, and chaparral shrubs dominate the surrounding hillsides. There was a proposal recently to construct a dam across Sespe Creek in a narrows downstream from the campground. The intent was to catch winter flood water and use it for irrigation, but the plan was dropped because the rock forming the cliff sides of the narrows was determined not to be strong enough to anchor a dam.

22 W.T. FASER COLD SPRINGS RANCH
MILEAGE = 18.5   MARKER = 28.91

This ranch on the south side of Sespe Creek was originally established by Wheeler Blumberg, who also operated Wheeler's Hot Springs Resort on the North Fork of Matilija Creek. He used the Sespe site as a hunting and fishing camp for guests from his hot spring facility. There was no road in the early days so guests traveled on horseback up the upper North Fork of Matilija Canyon and down the Sespe to Blumberg's lodge.

When Highway 33 was completed, the Hartman family purchased the site and it became known as the Lower Hartman Ranch. The family already owned a homestead on Abadi Creek near the head of the Sespe, which became known as the Upper Hartman Ranch. The Hartman family still owns the Abadi property, but some years ago they sold the lower ranch to W.T. Faser. It is now called the Faser Cold Springs Ranch, marked by an old stone house and some very tall incense cedars that were planted by the original owner.

23 THE GIANT TULE CREEK SLIDE   MILEAGE = 18.9

Just before the Tule Creek bridge, the highway crosses the Tule Creek fault. The rocks that occur on the upthrust on the south side of the fault are composed of Cozy Dell shale, which is realtively soft and often unstable. On February 7 of 1998, during a period of heavy rains, the hillside to the west of Highway 33 started to slide. Six days later, the *Ojai Valley News* reported that the slide was still active. In October of 1999, they reported that Caltrans was still working on landslide removal, and work was expected to be completed in December of 1999 so the

The Faser Cold Springs Ranch compound, with the Tule Creek slide visible at upper left

highway could finally be reopened.

The massive slide buried a 100 foot section of Highway 33 under a mass of rocks and mud 15 feet deep. Caltrans estimates that 2.7 million cubic yards of debris were removed. Bennett Construction Company of Fillmore and Santa Paula was the contractor on the $2.5 million cleanup. A fleet of 26 trucks hauled the debris to a dump site on private property, located five miles from the slide near Rose Valley.

The Tule Creek slide was four to five times as large as a previous slide that occurred on the northern side of Pine Mountain in 1993-1994, and closed the highway for over five months. The delay was attributed to a disagreement between the Forest Service and the Highway Department over what to do with the slide debris. Congressman Elton Gallegy helped to bring about a compromise.

After passing the slide you enter the area burned by the Wolf Fire, so named because it started at Wolf's Grill about ten miles up the highway. It is said that people were shooting tracer ammunition at an old truck behind the cafe, not aware that there was gas in the tank. The fire started on June 1 of 2002, spread very quickly, and burned over 21,645 acres.

The effects of the fire are visible on both sides of the road over the next ten miles. Chaparral, juniper, pinyon, and bigcone Douglas-fir burned high on the north wall of the canyon. Even creekside cottonwoods burned, because the fire followed an exceptionally dry winter and spring.

For a time the Matilija Wilderness and the Sespe Condor Sanctuary were threatened, but an intensive firefighting effort stopped the advance.

Some 70 years ago earlier, the enormous Matilija Fire burned some of the same area now blackened by the Wolf Fire. Highway 33 was under construction at the time, and many of the wooden stakes marking the route had to be replaced before construction could continue.

24 FORMER CIVILIAN CONSERVATION CORPS CAMP ⤙ MILEAGE = 19.2 ⤙ MARKER = 29.62 (BRIDGE)

Just past the Tule Creek slide, the road turns north along the west bank of Sespe Creek and crosses the Tule Creek bridge. The tule (pronounced too-lee) is a plant found in riparian areas throughout California. More commonly known as "cattail", the plant has both narrow and broadleaf varieties. The Chumash Indians used the leaves in twined mats and roof thatching, and used the rhizomes and pollen for food.

Rocks beyond the bridge are composed of Cozy Dell shale with some layers of sandstone. This formation is softer than the surrounding rock, and erodes more readily. Here erosion has created a flat area where a road camp was established during the construction of the highway. Later, in 1933, the Civilian Conservation Corps transformed the old facility into a CCC camp and stationed some 150 men there. With the outbreak of WWII, the CCC program came to an end. Subsequently the County of Ventura used the camp as a highway maintenance station until the early 1950's. Now a stand of trees planted during the CCC era and a bin of sand on stilts are all that mark the site. The Highway Department stores sand there to spread on the road when it is icy.

Just beyond the site (at 20.2 miles) the highway crosses Sespe Creek for the first and only time. This bridge marks the beginning of the Sespe Gorge.

25 SESPE GORGE ⤙ MILEAGE = 20.1 ⤙ MARKER = 30.52 (BRIDGE)

Sespe Gorge is a deep narrows through which Sespe Creek flows. The side walls of the gorge are composed of steeply dipping marine Middle Miocene Matilija sandstone in an east laying anticline.

This was one of the most difficult and expensive portions of the highway to construct. Large rocks still come crashing down on the highway after rains. A contract for $586,664.31 was awarded to Sharp and Associates in 1932 for this section, and it was completed in 1933.

A perennial flow of water is found in the gorge bottom, which is lined with riparian vegetation including white alders and black cottonwoods. The Spanish names for these trees, *aliso* and *alamo* respectively, figure in many local place names and always indicate the presence of significant ground water. Both trees are deciduous and turn a striking yellow as winter approaches. To the left of the highway on the north facing cliffs of the gorge, numerous bigcone Douglas-fir trees can be seen. The creek here has long been noted for its good trout fishing.

Highway 33 runs along the base of these ridges before entering the Sespe Gorge, right

A short distance into the gorge, a water gauge located on the canyon cliffside measures the volume of flow throughout the year. The north facing cliff at the gauge is a renowned site for rock climbing. Climbers can often be seen testing their skill on the canyon wall above the creek.

The Sespe Light and Power Company filed papers with the Forest Service and other affected government bodies on August 24, 1921, withdrawing plans for a dam in the Sespe Gorge. After extensive study, they had come to the conclusion that a dam would not store enough water to make the project profitable.

As the highway continues to climb, the Sespe Gorge widens into a valley where the open canyon bottom is covered with Great Basin sage and rabbit brush. One leaf pinyon pine and California juniper trees are seen on the hillsides, and will predominate for the remainder of the drive.

26 DERRY DALE CREEK
MILEAGE = 21.3 ⟿ MARKER = 31.72 (BRIDGE)

This creek drains the south side of Pine Mountain Ridge, passing through a wooded valley. It is not known why this name was given to this creek. "Derry" was used as a refrain or chorus in old time songs ("derry-down"). "Dale" refers to a small valley, usually wooded.

27 POTRERO JOHN CREEK AND TRAIL
MILEAGE = 21.7   MARKER = JUST PAST 32.00

Just after the highway crosses the bridge over Potrero John Creek, a sign on the right side of the road marks the trail that runs northward up this creek. The hike to Potrero John Campground is just over one and a half miles from the trailhead. A large oak tree located at a stream crossing marks the campground. Its species is known by at least three names: canyon oak, golden cup oak, or maul oak. It is composed of very hard wood that was once used to make mauls for splitting wood. There is a grate stove at the camp, and water is available from the creek.

The name was originally spelled "Jon", but was later changed to John. John Power lived in the area in the 1900's and pastured cattle in the canyon. *Potrero* is a Spanish word meaning "mountain meadow". The mountain ranges of Los Padres National Forest contain many potreros, which have been used historically as grazing areas for livestock.

The Lopez Homestead sits on the bank of Sespe Creek

28 MUNSON CREEK AND FAULT
MILEAGE = 23.5   MARKER = 33.80 (BRIDGE)

As the highway crosses the bridge over Munson Creek, it also crosses Munson Creek fault. The fracturing of the shale outcroppings and beds becomes more evident after the fault, which runs in an east-west direction for over fifty miles. Rock is visibly displaced along the fault for about one mile. It is believed that the fault was named for a geologist named Munson, who once mapped in this area.

29 LOPEZ HOMESTEAD   ⤳ MILEAGE = 25.2 ⤳ MARKER = 33.3

On October 15, 1891, Teodoro Lopez applied for a homestead patent on 160 acres located alongside Sespe Creek. He received his final certificate on January 8, 1891. The original cabin was destroyed in a fire and rebuilt by Emilio Ortega, former postmaster in Ventura.

The Canet Land and Cattle Company purchased the property and leased it to a number of Ventura residents. The site became known as Coyote Hole. The Bonsall family bought up all of the Canet holdings in the 1970's, and leases the Lopez property to the current resident.

30 THE OLD FRANK FELT RANCH
MILEAGE = 25.7 ⤳ MARKER = 35.82

Frank Felt was born in 1890 and passed away in 1968. In the early years of his life he lived in Los Angeles and worked in a series of business ventures, the last of which was selling Ortega chili peppers. In 1914 he developed a serious stomach ailment and had to have surgery. His doctor told him he would not live long unless he got away from the tensions of the business world.

Frank moved to Sespe Canyon and established a 160 acre homestead, where he lived on and off for over 41 years. One of the big joys in his life was playing the part of Father Salvedierra in the Ramona Pageant, an outdoor play based on a book written by Helen Hunt Jackson in 1894. He played the role from the founding of the pageant in 1923 until 1946.

During the pageant Frank always made a point of seeing Miss Ella Eggen. They fell in love, but Frank did not think any young lady would want to live at the end of the horse trail to his ranch; Highway 33 was not yet built. One day the dog began to bark and Frank looked out the cabin door and saw four horses coming up the trail. The first rider was the witness, the second was the minister, and the third was Ella leading a pack horse with all her belongings. It was Leap Year, and he said yes. They enjoyed a very secluded rural life until Highway 33 was constructed across their land just beyond their front door.

Frank Felt was known as the "sage of the Sespe". He wrote two books of poetry, *Songs of the Sespe* and *Sunset in the Sespe*, along with many other poems that were published in numerous publications. He used to make frames from native wood for his poems and sell them at Wheeler Hot Springs.

With advanced age creeping up, the Felts moved to Oxnard in 1956. The property was sold to Pardner Hicks, who operated a pack station where he took people on horseback trips into Los Padres National Forest. In 1999 new owners purchased the property, and have so far made few

The old Felt cabin was saved from the Wolf Fire by firefighters

changes to it. A sign reading "Al 'Louie' Schreiner", painted on a chipped and battered blade of an airplane propeller, is posted on the lefthand side of the front gate.

Howdy Stranger

Welcome stranger, at our door
Pass – as though you'd passed before.
Come tarry – ere your way you wend
And sip our cup as friend to friend.
Break freely of our humble crust
Departing friendly when you must.
Your station or your worldly pelf
Is naught – just smile and be yourself.
And to thyself, be staunchly true,
Our friends are made from folks like you.

- Frank D. Felt

# 31 CHORRO GRANDE CREEK AND TRAIL
MILEAGE = 26 (CREEK) & 26.5 (TRAIL)   MARKER = 36.13 (BRIDGE) & 36.6 (TRAIL)

Chorro Grande Creek descends the south face of Pine Mountain Ridge. It starts as a small stream at Chorro Grande Spring, and flows past Oak Camp before crossing Highway 33 and emptying into Sespe Creek. *Chorro* is Spanish for a gushing spring, referring to the water that gushes from under a large boulder in springtime to form the creek.

The Chorro Grande trail (23W05) begins one half mile west of the concrete bridge where the creek crosses the highway. After a very steep climb, the trail passes the spring and ends at Pine Mountain Campground, located on Forest Service Road 6N06 on the summit of Pine Mountain Ridge. It is best to hike down, and designate a driver to move the car from one end of the trail to the other.

During the 1970's, considerable exploration was carried out to develop a phosphate deposit in the Santa Margarita Formation along the Chorro Grande trail. Permission to mine the phosphate was not given because of the potential for environmental damage, as well as the danger posed by large trucks hauling the phosphate rock along Highway 33.

3 2 GODWIN CANYON   ⤺ MILEAGE = 27.4 ⤺ MARKER = 37.52

Mr. Godwin was in charge of the survey party that was surveying township lines in this part of the Sespe Valley in 1879. Godwin Canyon drains a part of the south face of Pine Mountain Ridge, crosses Highway 33, and joins Sespe Creek.

3 3 CHERRY CREEK CANYON
MILEAGE = 28.2 ⤺ MARKER = 38.22

The canyon received its name from the large number of wild cherry shrubs (*Prunus ilicifolia*) that grow in the chaparral on the hillsides of the upper canyon. The red fruit of the shrub, commonly known as holly-leaved cherry or islay, figured in many Chumash recipes and is much loved by our native black bears.

The canyon drains northward and empties into Sespe Creek. Originally the Upper North Fork trail of Matilija Canyon continued down the side of the creek to the Sespe, but in the 1960's the Ohio Oil Company built a dirt road on the trail to reach a drilling site. They came up with a dry hole.

Cherry Creek Road is closed seasonally due to the possible presence of spawning steelhead trout in the streams. The hillsides on either side of the road have long been used for target practice. The area is often littered with large amounts of trash in the form of abandoned targets, cans, and bottles. You can hike the road to reach the trailhead of the Upper North Fork of Matilija Creek. It also connects to the Ortega OHV motorcycle trail, which descends to end at Highway 33 north of Wheeler Gorge Campground.

Ortega Hill, located at the head of Cherry Creek, was named after Ramon Ortega. He ranched at Potrero Seco, at the head of Sespe Creek, in the 1860's. It is reported that he hunted and killed fifteen California grizzly bears in a single day at Potrero Seco, capturing them with a rawhide lasso.

Wolf's Grill as seen from Highway 33

34 WOLF'S GRILL (FORMERLY KNOWN AS PINE MOUNTAIN INN) ⸙ MILEAGE = 28.8 ⸙ MARKER = 38.81

The earliest known settler associated with this site was Juan Diego Arrellanes, who filed a claim on some of the property in 1897. Warren Felt moved to the Sespe area in 1920 because of lung problems he suffered after being gassed in WWI. He settled on the Arrellanes site, just up the canyon from his brother Frank Felt. Warren died in 1941 and the property passed through several hands, becoming for a time the site of the Pine Mountain Inn. The old farm equipment in front of the building came from the Ayers Ranch near Santa Paula.

In 1975, Tom Wolf of Oxnard retired from a teaching career and bought the Inn. He changed the name to Wolf's Pine Mountain Inn, and served a clientele made up of hunters, fishermen and "good old" Harley motorcycle groups. In recent years the Inn has become a popular destination for all types of motorcycle travelers on Highway 33. The small cafe became known for its accumulation of one dollar bills signed by customers and stuck to the ceiling and walls with chewing gum. At one point there were over four thousand in all. Mr. Wolf entertains customers with the story that the bills cover up bullet holes. The bills were finally taken down in 1996 when El Nino storms closed the highway for eight months, but a new collection is growing fast.

Wolf's Pine Mountain Inn usually closes from fall to spring. When open, the Inn serves sandwiches and drinks. Parties and barbecues can be scheduled.

35 ADOBE CANYON ⤶ MILEAGE = 29 ⤶ MARKER = 39.03

Highway 33 has been tending toward the west, but as it passes Wolf's Grill it makes a turn to the north and begins to climb up Adobe Canyon for about four miles. *Adobe* is the Spanish word for a heavy clay soil.

As you start up the canyon you pass between two massive outcroppings of Coldwater sandstone of the Eocene age. The exposed faces of the rock are pockmarked with numerous cavities due to water ande wind erosion. Beyond the Coldwater cliffs there is a large area of sandstone and clay stone of a reddish color; the rock of the Sespe Formation of the Oligocene age.

On the right side of the canyon just below a large sandstone outcropping is the site of the abandoned Sandstone Campground. Travelers used to stop and camp here in the 1930's, and a fire guard was stationed here during fire season. The campground was eventually closed because it was located on private property belonging to the Wagy Ranch.

An old photo of the Sandstone Campground, now closed

Further up, the canyon begins to narrow as it enters the Monterey Formation, which is composed of bands of gray to white shale. When this rock breaks down it becomes the clay soil that gives the canyon its name.

Across the canyon from the road, a cut has produced a visible scar. This is the route of the Casitas natural gas pipeline, which runs from the Cuyama oil fields to Oxnard and supplies natural gas to run a large electrical generating plant.

Growing along the creek bed are a large number of willow shrubs, while the hillsides and stream terrace are dominated by a dense stand of pinyon pines. The nuts from the cone of the pinyon pine are borne in some years in abundance. They mature in the early fall and provide food for wildlife. The Chumash Indians used the pinyon nuts as a staple in their diet. They also used the pitch from the tree as glue, and to waterproof the inside of their water bottles.

Near the head of the canyon are the sites of a couple of abandoned homesteads, and then the highway makes a leftward bend and begins to climb the face of Pine Mountain Ridge. In this bend there is often a prominent display of Matilija poppies. With its large white petals surrounding a yellow center, this local poppy is often called "fried-egg plant".

At the top of Pine Mountain the highway cuts through Sespe strata

The highway climbs up through Coldwater sandstone, and again enters the Sespe Formation. At the top of the grade on the left side, bent strata of Sespe rock are exposed in the road cut. The road over Pine Mountain Ridge was one of the most expensive parts of the Highway 33 construction. The work was done by C.T. Willis and Sons, Inc. for an estimated $27,000, but when this section was completed in 1931 the final cost came to over $300,000.

36 PINE MOUNTAIN SUMMIT
MILEAGE = 32.8   MARKER = JUST PAST 42.54

The highway reaches its highest point at Pine Mountain Summit, with an elevation of 5,080 feet. This ridgeline divides the Sespe River canyon to the south from the upper Cuyama River valley to the north. A number of bigcone Douglas-fir trees grow just north of the divide. In the winter, low clouds from the north often drift through the tall conifers and leave a coating of ice crystals on the needles, presenting a beautiful effect.

Two side roads branch off here at the summit. Beyond a locked gate on the lefthand side, Forest Service administrative road 6N03 leads west to Potrero Seco, and then south to Monte Arido, Murietta Saddle, and the upper Juncal area. On the right, Pine Mountain Road 6N06 climbs east along the crest of Pine Mountain Ridge, and leads to campgrounds and trailheads in the Reyes Peak area. This road was constructed in 1950 by Standard Oil to access the site of the Hattie Russell oil well. No oil was found.

A sign at the beginning of Pine Mountain Road gives the distance to Pine Mountain Campground and the Chorro Grande Trail. Reyes Peak Campground is also located on this road. Both campgrounds have six sites and are available on a first come first served basis. Neither camp has water. At the end of the road, the Pine Mountain Trail 23W04 begins. It leads to a junction with the Gene Marshall Piedra Blanca National Recreation Trail in the Sespe Wilderness. Pine Mountain Road is closed to vehicles in winter months due to the snow that accumulates on the summit, but in summer it is a great place to camp or picnic.

37 PINE MOUNTAIN FAULT
MILEAGE = 33.6　　MARKER = JUST PAST 43.12

The Pine Mountain fault crosses the highway about 200 feet beyond highway marker 43.12. As you begin to descend northward from Pine Mountain Summit, there are two steep rock exposures close to each other on the right. The first shows sandstone and shale beds dipping mostly southward, and the second shows shale beds in an almost vertical expression. This is the Pine Mountain fault, with Matilija sandstone on the north of it and Cozy Dell shale on the south. This is a south thrusting fault that is traceable for about 35 miles from Bear Creek Canyon to Piru Canyon, mostly along the south face of Pine Mountain Ridge. There is a vertical displacement of several thousand feet on the north side of the fault.

38 UPPER CUYAMA VALLEY OVERLOOK
MILEAGE = 34.5　　MARKER = 44.43

A large parking area is situated on the north side of the highway at 4,500 feet elevation. In the wintertime, the highway department uses the overlook as a temporary dump site for rocks and mud that have fallen onto the highway. They remove the debris in spring and use it for fill elsewhere. Matilija poppies, rabbit brush and silk tassel grow on the edges of the parking area.

Looking northward from the overlook, the south flank of the San Emigdio Mountains is visible in the far distance. From left to right the peaks are: Mount Abel or Cerro Noroeste, Grouse Mountain, Sawmill Mountain, and Mount Pinos. With an elevation of 8,831 feet, Mount Pinos is the tallest mountain in the southern Los Padres National Forest.

The Cuyama Overlook is a good place to rest and enjoy the view

At the base of the range, you see San Emigdio Mesa and the Cuyama Badlands. These badlands are composed of non-marine sediments that have been dissected by the headwaters of Apache and Dry canyons to form eroded areas much like those of Bryce Canyon. Fossil bones of extinct mammals have been found in some of the exposed layers of clay. Directly below the overlook, a canyon runs east-west along the Big Pine Fault.

39 BIG PINE FAULT ⁓ MILEAGE = 36.3 ⁓ MARKER = 46.00

Continuing northward, Highway 33 makes a big horseshoe curve below the Cuyama overlook. The Big Pine Fault crosses the road in this bend. The south slope of this fault canyon is composed of Cozy Dell shale, while the north slope is composed of Juncal rocks. We last encountered the Juncal Formation at the Santa Ynez fault, below Wheeler Gorge Campground.

Big Pine Fault was named in 1925 by R. N. Nelson, and mapped by Diblee and Hall in the early 1950's. It is an east west trending left slip fault and extends for about 50 miles. Its eastern end joins with the San Andreas fault at Lake of the Woods, east of Lockwood Valley. It has been proposed that the Garlock Fault, east of the San Andreas fault, was at one time an extension of the Big Pine Fault.

Because of surface fractures, it is proposed that the Big Pine Fault was the source of a major earthquake in 1852. Stream offsets along the fault have been estimated to measure as much as

3,000 feet. There is a 4,000 foot elevation sign at 36.5 miles as the highway runs east-west along the fault.

40 BEAR CREEK AND DEAL TRAIL
MILEAGE = 37.8 ⤳ MARKER = 47.47

The highway rounds a ridge on the north side of the Big Pine Fault as it exits the fault canyon and enters Bear Canyon. On the left side of the highway a Forest Service sign marks the start of the Deal Trail (24W04) and informs you that Mine Camp is 2 miles away, and Deal Junction is 6.5 miles. A large concentration of coffee berry (*Rhamnus californica*) shrubs grow at the trailhead, quite attractive with their red fruit in season. It is said that early miners mixed the dried fruit of this shrub with their real coffee grounds as an extender.

The trail up Bear Creek is very pretty, as it passes through a narrows that often has a small amount of water flowing under large oaks and bigcone Douglas-firs. After about 2 miles the canyon widens and an old abandoned dirt road leads eastward to Mine Camp. The main trail continues up Bear Creek, and climbs over a divide to steeply descend into Deal Canyon. Mr. Deal was prospecting for uranium, but he never found any. From Deal Junction, the Rancho Nuevo Trail (24W03) can be followed either downstream to Rancho Nuevo Camp and Highway 33, or upstream to Upper Rancho Nuevo Camp.

In the days before Highway 33 was constructed, this trail up Bear Creek was the route between Potrero Seco and Ozena. Currently, the proposed Condor National Recreation Trail is routed up Bear Creek.

41 OZENA FOREST SERVICE FIRE STATION
MILEAGE = 38.7

The name "Ozena" comes from *ocena*, a Spanish word for rhinitis, which is an inflammation of the nose lining. It probably refers to a condition caused by the pollen from local plants.

A picnic area and drinking water are available at the Ozena Forest Service Fire Station, which was once the site of a homestead. Peter Herlick filed a claim on this property in 1892 and received his patent certificate in 1899. He reconveyed the property back to the government in 1904.

While serving as a forest ranger from 1900 to 1931, J.D. Reyes maintained the Cuyama Forest Service District office at his residence on the mesa above the present Ozena Campground on Lockwood Valley Road. When J.D. retired from the Forest Service, the station was moved to the former Herlick homestead alongside the newly completed Highway 33. Eventually the Cuyama Forest Service District was merged with the Mount Pinos Forest Service District, and the ranger station became a fire station. Ozena Station will be one of the trailheads on the proposed Condor National Recreation Trail. Hikers heading east will travel up Boulder Canyon, while

Cone shaped native incense cedars mark the Ozena Station

westbound hikers will travel on the Bear Canyon and Deal Canyon trails. When completed, this section of the Condor Trail will cross Los Padres National Forest from Piru Creek in Ventura County to Nira Campground in Santa Barbara County.

North of the station on the right side, road cuts begin to expose the terrestrial Quatal Formation, laid down during the Pliocene Age in ancient lake beds. On the left side of the road is a low hillside composed of marine Juncal Formation, the same formation we saw at the tunnels on the North Fork of Matilija Creek. The rock formations are influenced by the Ozena fault, which crosses Highway 33 a short distance north of the station.

42 JUNCTION OF HIGHWAY 33 AND LOCKWOOD VALLEY ROAD ⌒ MILEAGE = 38.8

A sign marks this junction and informs you that Lockwood Valley lies 18 miles to the east. The road continues on past Lake of the Woods and Frazier Park, and ends 35 miles from this junction at Interstate 5. A short distance up Lockwood Valley Road on the right is the site of the historic Wagy Ranch, where in 1933 an estimated 35,000 people attended a large barbecue to celebrate the completion and opening of Highway 33, then known as the Maricopa Road.

Further up the road on the right side, Ozena Campground provides a good camping and picnic location with ten tables and stoves under very large old cottonwood trees. There is a pit toilet and no water at the campground.

On the right side of the road just before the Cuyama River ford is the site of the Reyes Ranch. The family established the ranch in 1851, when Rafael Reyes and his brothers drove 2,000 head of cattle and 1,000 horses over Tejon Pass into the upper Cuyama Valley. They were the first residents to establish a home in this area. A wooden structure has been built onto the original Reyes adobe, and the building is still in use.

43 CUYAMA RIVER BRIDGE   MILEAGE = 39

The Cuyama River is formed by the junction of several canyons that drain the north slope of the Pine Mountain Ridge. At first the river flows to the west. After passing under the Cuyama River bridge, it turns and flows north until it reaches the main Cuyama Valley. Here it turns again and flows westward to Twitchell Reservoir, eventually joining the Sisquoc River near Santa Maria. At this point the two rivers become the Santa Maria River, which reaches the ocean at Guadalupe Dunes.

This bridge was rebuilt in 1999, and is the only one across the upper Cuyama River. Every so often flash floods race down the river bed, but much of the year the Cuyama River is just a small stream of water that eventually sinks into the sand. Willow thickets and buffalo berry shrubs grow along this part of the river, but are often washed away by flooding. Cottonwood trees stand further back from the river's edge, and juniper and pinyon pine trees grow up the slopes of the wide wash.

44 LOS PADRES NATIONAL FOREST ROAD 7N04 (DICK SMITH WILDERNESS)
MILEAGE = 40.5   MARKER = JUST PAST 50.00

A Forest Service sign marks this dirt road that branches off on the left side of the highway and soon fords the Cuyama River. The crossing is not passable when the river is flowing strongly after rain. The road continues up an open valley and splits. The left fork goes 1.5 miles to Rancho Nuevo Camp, the trailhead to Deal Junction and Upper Rancho Nuevo Camp in the Dick Smith Wilderness. The first mile of this trail winds through a beautiful narrow canyon with high, heavily weathered cliffs on either side. The right fork follows up a dry canyon through a forest of pinyon pines to Tinta Camp, a distance of 3 miles. There is no water at the campsites and the primitive facilities are often vandalized.

From Tinta Camp, an off-road motorcycle trail continues up Tinta Canyon. It passes by the road to Cuyama Lookout on Cuyama Peak, and eventually descends Dry Canyon Road to the Forest Service Buckhorn Road in Santa Barbara Canyon.

45 APACHE SCHOOL SITE   ⤴ MILEAGE = 40.5

On the left side of the Los Padres National Forest Road 7N04, between Highway 33 and the Cuyama River crossing, is a half circle of Monterey cypress and other shade trees. In the center once stood the Apache School.

The last teacher was Mrs. Nellie Stannard, who came to the school from the Los Angeles area. After being widowed in 1928 with three children, she married Mr. Edward Overton, who had three daughters. Nellie was not able to find a teaching job in Los Angeles, and learned that the Apache School in the upper Cuyama needed a teacher - provided there were five students enrolled. There were only two local children, so the school was about to close. Nellie's six children brought the class size up to eight, and she was hired by the Ventura School District. Her contract paid about $1,000 for the first year. An old abandoned school on the site was offered as both residence and classroom. There was no inside water or toilet, and a barbecue was used for cooking.

The Overton family lived there for several years and made many improvements, such as planting the trees that mark the site. Eventually enough of the children reached high school age that the number again fell below the required five students, and the school was closed. The family moved to Maricopa.

The county school had an agreement with the Forest Service, which owned the land, that if the school was closed all the facilities had to be removed. This was done, and later a community center was established on the site. Use of the center came to an end when many of the families moved away. The building was moved to the Ventucopa Forest Station, leaving only the trees that had been planted around three sides of the school.

Most of this information and much more came from a letter one of the Overton daughters, Emily S. Levine, wrote to Jim Blakley about her childhood by the Cuyama River.

46 HALF WAY STATION   ⤴ MILEAGE = 41.2

This roadside café got its name from being located halfway between Ojai and Taft on Highway 33. The Half Way Station serves sandwiches along with cold beer, wine, and distilled spirits. It opens at 10:00 a.m. Friday through Tuesday, and is closed Wednesdays and Thursdays. Monday night features free spaghetti and garlic bread dinner for all comers.
Construction started on the facility in 1948 when Tom Griffin sold ten acres to Lee Theris. Theris built the café and added a gas pump, but gas is no longer available. He also moved a tin building to the site from Maricopa.

At present the café walls are decorated with over 500 hats and caps, along with hundreds of humorous bumper stickers. The proprietor is Harlan D. Lingo, who also owns a ranch across the Cuyama River from the Station. The Station has no phone, but does have radio communications to the outside world. The address is 28511 Maricopa Highway, Maricopa 93252

The Half Way Station stands at the midpoint between Ojai and Taft

# 47 POP'S PLACE AND CASTLE CANYON AREA
MILEAGE = 41.5   MARKER = 50.71

Beginning just north of the Half Way Station, the highway crosses four bridges over small dry canyons. South to north, they are: Castle Creek, Round Spring Canyon Creek, Corral Canyon, and Oak Creek.

Just past the Castle Creek bridge stands what is left of "Pop's Place". The old white wooden building is still intact, though much the worse for the weathering. The small store with one gas pump, located 40 miles from Ojai and 42 miles from Maricopa, was one of the first commercial enterprises in the upper Cuyama.

"Pop" George Robertson operated it up to the age of 84, with the aid of his talking dog "Cry-Baby". Walt Harrington lived close by, and was a very good friend. They finally moved in together and spent their last years under the same roof. Local residents referred to them as the "Cuyama Kids", and nicknamed the store the "Country Club".

In the 1940's you could buy a bottle of beer from Pop for 15 cents, but his specialty was making rattlesnake necklaces. He cleaned the vertebral bones, strung them alternating with glass beads, and sold the necklaces.

Two tenths of a mile south of the Corral Canyon bridge, the Ozena fault trace is exposed where

The remains of the building once known as Pop's Place

it crosses the highway. It is a thrust fault and dips about 45 degrees southwest, uplifting marine strata over the younger terrestrial formations. This fault extends 25 miles north to where it intersects the Big Pine Fault.

According to an old Forest Service status report sheet, a right of way was dedicated on March 19, 1910 for the Bakersfield and Ventura Railroad. At this point it would have run close to the present highway. It was proposed to start at Sunset or Midway south of Taft, run up the valley over the mountains, and end at the ocean near Ventura. J.W. Burson and H.M. Rossell were the promoters of the project. No work was ever done on the route, except on paper.

# 48 APACHE CANYON
MILEAGE = 44.5 ⤺ MARKER = 53.80 (BRIDGE)

This name is applied to several locations in this part of Ventura County. It has been suggested that in the early days of the Reyes family, they employed an Apache Indian as a cowboy on ranch property they owned in the canyon. Another possible source of the name is found in an 1819 report by Father Senan, who claimed that "Mohave Apache Indians" raided this area and caused extensive damage.

Historian and ethnologist J.P. Harrington reported that gold was once panned in the upper part of Apache Canyon. At present, a graded dirt road runs up the canyon for nine and a half miles to reach Nettle Springs Campground. The road ends with a loop under some large scattered pinyon pines. There are four campsites with tables and firepits, but no water other than a small flow from the spring that soon sinks into the sandy wash. Further up Apache Canyon, in the heart of the Cuyama Badlands, a trail leads through castellated, banded rock formations reminiscent of Bryce Canyon. Remains of horse, camel and other ancient fossil bones can be found in the eroded walls.

About a mile and a half north of the mouth of Apache Canyon and one mile east of Highway 33 is a very large anticline where the Richfield Oil Company drilled Apache Unit Number One oil well. It was drilled 10,562 feet deep, but no oil was found.

Just past Apache Canyon (at 45.1 miles) is an interesting plant found here on the extreme northern edge of its natural range. The *Opuntia parryi* is a cholla cactus often known as "valley cholla" or "cane cholla". It grows locally on canyonside slopes in a few scattered colonies with Great Basin sage and other shrubs. At this spot, a small group of the cholla plants grows on the east side of the highway. The large green shrub in front of the cactus, with its small yellow flowers and spiny fruit, is a member of the gooseberry group.

49 MORRO HILL   MILEAGE = 44.5

Morro Hill with the Cuyama River in the foreground

Morro Hill is located on the west side of the Cuyama River across from the mouth of Apache Canyon. In Spanish the word *morro* means a steep sided, cone shaped hill. El Morro rises 500 feet above the riverbed. It is composed of Tertiary Caliente Conglomerate formation.

On June 29, 1908 the Forest Service passed an order to establish an administrative site just south of Morro Hill. The hundred acre site, located on a terrace on the west bank of the Cuyama River, was used to pasture Forest Service horses. On November 22, 1913 the Forest Service revoked the order, as they had started using automobiles instead of horses.

50 BRUBAKER CANYON
MILEAGE = 45.6　　MARKER = JUST PAST 56.00

In 1918 members of the Brubaker family filed homesteads that included a canyon on the west side of the Cuyama River, which came to be known by the family name. On the lefthand side of Highway 33, a dirt road marked by a mailbox crosses the Cuyama River and leads to the old Brubaker property. From there, a Forest Service road used to run up Brubaker Canyon to a fire tower located on top of Cuyama Peak. The road crossed private land and was eventually closed by the property owner.

A little further up the highway (at 47.1 miles) a roadside sign informs you that you are leaving Los Padres National Forest.

51 BURGES CREEK BRIDGE
MILEAGE = 48.2　　MARKER = 57.21

The creek is named for Mr. J.B. Berges, who filed a homestead claim in the canyon in 1896, and for Mr. A. Berges who filed a claim in 1897. Over time the spelling has changed to its current form. Burges Canyon Road, a private ranch road, extends up this canyon to the Black Ranch and dead ends about a half mile beyond it. The Black Ranch was homesteaded in 1915 by Mermin M. Black.

Just past the Burges Creek bridge, a roadside sign announces that you are crossing the north-south line that divides Ventura and Santa Barbara counties. For the next few miles the highway will be in Santa Barbara County, and shortly before the end of this tour it will cross into San Luis Obispo County. The Kern County line is just a few miles to the east.

52 COMMUNITY OF VENTUCOPA　　MILEAGE = 50

Ventucopa was established as a town around the time of WWI, when sections of government land were opened for late homesteading. Several families from Carpinteria homesteaded claims near the new townsite. They shipped their household property to Maricopa by Southern Pacific railroad, and then rode on horseback over the mountains to the Cuyama Valley.

Ventucopa got its name by virtue of being located between Ventura and Maricopa. Homesteaders had to travel twenty three miles to Maricopa to buy provisions. The round trip took sixteen hours on horseback.

At the present time, Ventucopa is a community of small ranches with no public services available. Many descendents of the original settlers still live there.

53 QUATAL CANYON AND PATO CANYON
MILEAGE = 50.3 AND 50.6

The highway crosses Quatal Creek with an unnamed bridge at 50.3 miles. At 50.6 miles, Quatal Canyon Road turns off to the right. *Guata* is a California Spanish term for juniper tree, and *guatal* is a place where junipers grow. The derivation, *quatal*, is an apt name for this canyon that passes through miles of pinyon-juniper forest as it climbs in elevation toward the northwestern base of Cerro Noroeste.

Quatal Canyon Road is a rough, Forest Service dirt road that extends eastward up the canyon along the north side of the Chumash Wilderness. It joins Cerro Noroeste Road just north of Toad Spring. From this point, Mil Potrero Highway can be followed eastward to Interstate 5.

Rocks exposed at the mouth of the canyon are of the Terrestrial Morales formation. During the 1940's and 1950's, gypsum found within the Pliocene Quatal Formation was quarried a short distance up the canyon on the north side. The beds were two miles in length and ten to thirty feet deep. The gypsum was used in manufacturing plaster.

On the west side of the Cuyama River, across the highway from Quatal Canyon, is the mouth of Pato Canyon. A man by the name of Mr. Duck filed a homestead in the upper part of the canyon. When the U.S.G.S. mapped the area they gave Spanish names to known locations. They did not know that the canyon was named for a man rather than a bird, so they gave it the name *Pato*, which is the Spanish word for "duck".

54 SAGEBRUSH ANNIE'S CAFE   MILEAGE = 51.3

Sagebrush Annie's is a small wooden building originally built in 1948 as a grocery store. At one time it also housed the post office for the upper Cuyama Valley. Later it became a bar, and was named "The Diamond Belle" after a famous frontier establishment in Durango, Colorado.

In the mid-1980's the Diamond Belle was bought by Ron and Meg Emord. They renamed it Sagebrush Annie's Café and began to cater to members of the Professional Rodeo Cowboys Association. The Emords developed an arena and hosted rodeo events that drew competitors from all across the country. When they sold the restaurant the rodeo events came to an end.

Current owners Larry and Corrine have upgraded Sagebrush Annie's into a fine steakhouse that

40

features local wines. The cafe is open Thursday through Sunday nights starting at 5:00 p.m. Reservations are not required but it's a good idea to call first. The number is (661) 766-2319.

Sagebrush Annie's serves gourmet meals and local wines

5 5 "THE PLACE" RESTAURANT   ⤺ MILEAGE = 51.7

The Place was established in 1929 by Pearl Parady, who traded a 160 acre homestead for the property on the west side of Highway 33 at an elevation of 2,999 feet. At one time it was the site of one of the first post offices in the upper Cuyama Valley.

Wen and Gayle Carpenter bought The Place in 1973 and have operated it ever since. It is a family restaurant that serves breakfast, lunch and dinner. It is popular for serving cold beer in the hot days of summer. The walls are lined with a large collection of pin-on buttons representing many years of campaign slogans and jokes.

The Place is open from 9 a.m. to 7 p.m. every day but Tuesday. The Carpenters can be reached at (661) 766-2660. There is a pay phone outside near the front door that is available 24 hours a day.

5 6 BARNWOOD VINEYARD   ⤺ MILEAGE = 52

The site of the former Barnwood Vineyard is not currently open to the public.

The Place serves cold drinks and hot meals

# 5 7 SANTA BARBARA PISTACHIO COMPANY
MILEAGE = 53

The Santa Barbara Pistachio Company is located on the west side of Highway 33 about 6 miles south of its junction with Highway 166. It began in 1990 as a small roadside stand that Phyllis Harrington started beside Highway 33 to sell her locally grown pistachios. The business grew quickly, and in 1994 the Harrington and Zannon families constructed the present shop. The two families produce the pistachios on more than 700 acres, and then process and market them. Their specialty is flavored pistachios, which are hot-air roasted daily and are available in garlic, hot pepper, hickory, and onion & garlic varieties. The fresh nuts are sold at the roadside store, which also serves snacks and beverages in a small cafe. The store has picnic tables, a bathroom and the only gas station on this section of Highway 33.

5 8 VENTUCOPA RANGER STATION   MILEAGE = 53.5

This complex on the left side of the highway was originally the maintenance facility for the Cuyama District of Los Padres National Forest. When the district was combined with the Mount Pinos Ranger District, the facility was closed to the public.

The ranger station was started by the Hickey brothers in the early 1930's, after J.D. Reyes retired. It was first called Root Camp after a local rancher named George Root who worked part time for the Forest Service as a summer fire guard. Travelers used to camp there on their way to Maricopa. During the Depression era a Civilian Conservation Corps camp was constructed on the site. The present facility was built by the Forest Service.

Across Highway 33 from the station was an airfield that was used during WWII in emergencies when the main base in Bakersfield was blanketed with fog. The Forest Service practiced airdrops for supplying fire camps by dropping 5 gallon water cans onto a target on the airfield.

5 9 FORMER STUTZ CAFE   ⌒ MILEAGE = 54.4

Eugene Stutz had a popular cafe at this location in the 1930's

A series of stone and brick posts in a modern ranchyard on the east side of Hwy 33 is all that remains of the original Stutz Cafe. Eugene Stutz came to the Cuyama Valley in 1930 and homesteaded 390 acres in Santa Barbara Canyon. He then bought 160 additional acres that included highway frontage, and built a roadside cafe in 1934. He would make trips to Taft for supplies, leaving early in the morning before the frozen mud roadbed melted, and returning at night after the road had refrozen. In 1941 he moved his operation to the newly established town of Cuyama on Highway 166. Local farmers had begun to grow potatoes in the valley, and asked Mr. Stutz to relocate his cafe to accommodate the agricultural workers as well as the Cuyama oil field workers. Stutz's Cafe was popular for its fried chicken dinners. The cafe was also the seat of the Cuyama Post Office, and Mr. Stutz was postmaster from 1941 to 1953.

Currently Gene Stutz still lives on the site of the original cafe, which was taken down in 1948.

6 0 Ballinger Canyon Road   ⤙ Mileage = 56

This canyon is thought to be named after an early resident. Geraldo and Annie Reyes had a ranch at the head of the canyon for many years. Eventually they sold the ranch and opened a small cafe and service station at Grosser Grade, at the intersection of Highway 166 and Soda Lake Road.

A short distance up Ballinger Canyon Road is the Song Dog Ranch, named for the coyotes that serenade early in the mornings. Jim Reveley owns and operates the 164 acre ranch that contains a 40 acre campground, a lodge, picnic areas, and hiking and biking trails. Song Dog Ranch provides camping experiences for couples, families, and groups. You can bring your own gear and food, or try Song Dog's package that includes camping gear, barbecue and briquettes, and an ice chest stocked with good things to eat and drink. Reservations are required - call (800) 766-2461 or (661) 766-2454, or write Mr. Reveley at P.O. Box 175, New Cuyama, CA 93254.

The ranch hosts three rallies for motorcyclists each year with live music and plenty of food and drink. It is also the home of REV Packs, a type of soft luggage made for motorcyclists. The specialized motorcycle accessories are all made in a barn on the property.

Further up Ballinger Canyon, 3 1/2 miles from Highway 33, the road ends at a Forest Service campground. Ballinger Campground serves as a parking area and trailhead for off-road motorcycles and other vehicles. There are limited camping facilities, but no water is available.

6 1 Santa Barbara Canyon Road   ⤙ Mileage = 56

Santa Barbara Canyon serves as a route of access to Los Padres National Forest, in particular the Dick Smith and San Rafael Wildernesses. All-weather access to the canyon is from Highway 166, but Santa Barbara Canyon Road actually originates at Highway 33, although there is no sign to indicate the turnoff. The unmarked dirt road branches off Highway 33 in a southwesterly direction and crosses the Cuyama River without benefit of a bridge. This route is not recommended for cars. It is sandy when dry, and impassable when the river is high or muddy.

A few miles up the canyon, the road passes through the historic Santa Barbara Canyon Ranch, which was once the site of a Chumash village. The area was homesteaded in the early1800's, and is still a working cattle ranch. The original homestead land is now completely surrounded by Los Padres National Forest.

6 2 Foothill Road (County Line)   ⤙ Mileage = 56.9

Foothill Road starts at Highway 33 and runs in a westerly direction along the foothills of the Sierra Madre Mountains, which form the southern boundary of the Cuyama Valley. Foothill Road traces the county line between Santa Barbara and San Luis Obispo counties until it reaches the Cuyama River. This line also served as the southern boundary of Cuyama No. 2, the last land grant given by Mexico before California was taken over by the United States. The bridge at the river crossing washed out several years ago and vehicles must now cross the wide sandy river-bed, or go a long way around when the water is high.

6 3 THE WHITENER PLACE ⌐ MILEAGE = 58.5

The stone building on the right side of Highway 33 just before the junction with Highway 166 was built in the 1930's by James Whitener, who operated it as a dance hall. Helen Moore played the piano and Johnny Blanco played banjo. It was closed down during World War II due to problems on the premises, when fights broke out between oil field workers from Maricopa and Cuyama Valley residents.

Jim Whitener's son Buddy went to school in Maricopa with one of the girls from the Apache School, and they eventually married. Soon after the birth of their first child, Buddy was killed in an auto accident. His widow cooked for the C.C.C. Camp, then moved out of the valley to parts unknown.

The Whitener building sits just north of a small house that is currently in use. Following a fire in the early 1970's, all that remains of the old dance hall are the empty stone walls.

This structure was once the site of Whitener's popular dance hall

# 6 4 JUNCTION OF HIGHWAYS 33 AND 166
MILEAGE = 59.6

Our journey ends here where Highway 33 connects with Highway 166. A road sign gives the following distances: west to New Cuyama 10 and Santa Maria 70; north to Maricopa 14 and Bakersfield 60. On the west side of Highway 33 a sign gives the mileage southbound : Ojai 59 and Ventura 72.

From this junction, Highways 33 and 166 merge together as one road bearing both numbers, which heads northeast as far as the town of Maricopa, where the "Maricopa Road" portion of Highway 33 reaches its terminus. From Maricopa, Highway 33 continues north up the San Joaquin Valley almost all the way to Stockton, and Highway 166 can be traveled eastward to Interstate 5.

From its junction with Highway 33, Highway 166 runs westward to the ocean. It follows the Cuyama Valley and passes through the towns of Cuyama and New Cuyama. The highway runs alongside the Cuyama River and crosses over Twitchell Reservoir, where the Cuyama River bends south to flow into the Santa Maria River. The highway maintains its westward direction and eventually merges with Highway 101 just north of Santa Maria. A few miles south, Highway 166 splits off and continues west to end at its junction with Highway 1 in Guadalupe.

Travelers can keep going straight ahead 6 miles to the road's end at Guadalupe Dunes, where the Santa Maria River flows into the Pacific Ocean.

Acknowledgements

Allbright, Robert, *Cuyama Valley Yesterday and Today*. RGA Publishing Company, 1990.

Bates, Earl: "Ojai Valley News" articles and *Ojai Valley Visitors Guide*

Blakley, E.R. and Karen Barnette, *Historical Overview of Los Padres National Forest*. U.S.D.A. Forest Service, 1985.

Brantingham, Barney, "Around the County" columns. *Santa Barbara News Press*, 1986.

Diblee, Tom: Geology Maps of the area. Diblee Geological Foundation, 1985-2002.

Gray, Robert and Stephen Newswanger: *Historical Tour Guidebook; Mt. Pinos and Ojai Ranger Districts*. Los Padres Interpretive Association, 1981.

Gudde, Erwin G., *California Place Names; The Origin and Etymology of Current Geographical Names*. 4th ed. University of California Press, 1998.

Wegis, Virginia, "The Cuyama Kids." *Cuyama Valley News*.

Unknown Author, *The Cuyama Buckhorn Presents the Cuyama Valley; A Brief History and Points of Interest*.

Our thanks to the following who provided information:

Greg Wilkerson; U.S.D.I. Bureau of Land Management, Bakersfield Office
Ojai Valley Historical Society and Museum
Automobile Club of Southern California, Ventura County
Jim Blakley Jr. and Bonnie Blakley
Lil Clary
John Fritsche
Emily S. Levine
Donald Mills
Tom Wolf
Jim Reveley
Michael Zolkoski

INDEX

NOTES